じゃれマガ

100 Stories of 2019

from the email magazine
by Douglas S. Jarrell
ダグラス・ジャレル

浜島書店

INTRODUCTION

The stories of 2019 will remind you of the big changes that took place in Japan over the year. In May, Heisei turned to Reiwa when the Japanese emperor Akihito abdicated and his son Naruhito came to the throne. Another big change came in October when the consumption tax went up from 8% to 10%. While Japanese welcomed the new emperor, most people were unhappy about the extra 2% tax.

Most of the stories in this book were written by me, but there were many active readers who sent me stories. You will find some of them here, stories from all over Japan and even from abroad. I'm sure you will enjoy them. I want to encourage more readers to send in your stories. Although I can't post all of them on Readers' Corner, I certainly enjoy reading every one!

Finally, I want to thank the people who make this book possible: my wife Toshiko, the staff of Hamajima Shoten, and Ozaki Kanako, who has been illustrating the Jaremaga books since 2012. It is with great sadness that I inform you of her death. Kanako passed away at the beginning of March 2020. She was much too young to die, and I will always remember the beautiful smile she greeted me with whenever we met. She spent the last few months of her life in the hospital, but she worked hard until the end drawing most of the illustrations in this book. Please treasure these last creations of hers!

Douglas Jarrell

ジャレル先生の朗読音声を聞こう！
　本書の内容をジャレル先生自身の朗読で聞くことができます。次のホームページにアクセスして，ご利用ください。
http://catchawave.jp/jm/sound2019.html

（2020年6月公開予定）

INDEX

Sunrise, Food and Resolutions

The New Year's vacation is over now. How did you spend it? Did you get up early and see the first sunrise of the year? I did! Did you eat any Japanese New Year's food? I only ate rice cakes, but my students told me that they ate *datemaki* (a rolled sweet omelet), *kurikinton* (sweetened mashed sweet potatoes and chestnuts), and *ozoni* (rice cakes in soup). If you were watching TV, you probably saw the Hakone Ekiden, a long-distance relay race from Tokyo to Hakone and back. I saw some highlights. Did you make any New Year's resolutions? My resolution is to read one book a week.

resolution　決意，(新年の)誓い

僕はおせち料理はそれほど食べませんが，年末にお寺まで餅をつきに行きます。のし餅も作って，しばらくそれを家で食べていました。新年の決意は上の通り毎週本を1冊読むことでしたが，なかなか達成は難しかったです。それでも例年より多くの本を読めたのでよかったです。

High School and University at the Same Time!

A 16-year-old boy will graduate from high school and university at the same time this year. How can he do it? He goes to high school in his hometown in Kansas, which is in the middle of the U.S., and he studies online at Harvard University, which is about 2,600 kilometers away in the Boston area. When he was in elementary school, his parents found out that he was much more intelligent than most people. He began to feel unhappy and needed a challenge, so he started taking classes at Harvard. In May, he will graduate from high school, and then, two weeks later, he will graduate from Harvard. He wants to become a politician.

graduate from 〜　　〜を卒業する　　politician　政治家

 この少年は，普通の少年と同じようにゲームやスポーツに興味があり，部活でディベートをやりながら，高校の勉強と大学の勉強を同時に進めました。それができたのは彼の天才的な才能だけでなく，勤勉さと努力のおかげだと彼の高校の校長先生は言います。

The Best and the Worst

What are the 10 best movies of the year? You can find a list on the Internet. What about the 10 worst movies? You can find a list of them on the Internet, too. I look at the good movie list first, but I am always curious about the bad ones. I was surprised to see that the latest Jurassic Park movie made the list of the worst movies this time. I saw the first Jurassic Park movie when it came out in 1993, and it was great! It had everything: a great story, computer graphics (CG), and stars. This is the fifth movie. I guess the story isn't very good, and the dinosaurs are no longer exciting.

be curious about 〜　〜について知りたがる
make the list　（リストに）載る

インターネット上のリストを作成する人たちと僕の趣味が合わないこともあるので，一番良いと思う映画は必ずしも一致しませんが，悪いと思う映画は結構合う気がします。僕は最初の「ジュラシック・パーク」は好きだけど，この5作目は見に行きませんでした。

An Important Day for Families

I slept late in the morning on New Year's Day. I don't think I have ever seen the first sunrise. I ate *ozoni*. We put green and white square rice cakes in the soup. There are many shapes and colors of rice cakes depending on the region. I love it, but I don't like *osechi* because you have to eat the same things for days. I think nowadays there are few families who cook all the New Year's food by themselves. Anyway, New Year's Day is an important day for Japanese families to get together, like Christmas is for Christians.

(Written by a reader, Inui Aina)

region 地域　　for days 数日間　　Christian キリスト教徒

この読者が書いたように、日本のお正月とアメリカのクリスマスは雰囲気が似ていますが、クリスマスに家族と一緒に過ごす時間は1日(12月25日)または2日間(12月24日と25日)だけです。残り物を食べることはありますが、おせちのように数日間同じものを食べることはありません。

He Keeps on Going!

Some athletes just keep on going, and Miura Kazuyoshi is one of them. He has just signed a contract to play another year of professional soccer. That makes him one of the oldest professional soccer players in history. He went to Brazil when he was 15 years old because he wanted to play soccer, and he made his debut at the age of 19. He was already playing professional soccer when the J.League started. He has been playing professionally for more than 30 years! It must be rough playing with so many young players, but I hope he has a great season.

keep on going　進み続ける　　rough　つらい

 三浦知良選手がいなければ，今の日本のプロサッカーはなかったと言っても過言ではありません。彼は高校中退後，自分の夢を追うために1人でサッカー大国のブラジルへ渡った勇気ある少年でした。その後，日本サッカー界の最初のスーパースターとなり，Jリーグと日本代表に大きく貢献しました。

A Perfect Circle

I wish I were visiting my sister in New Hampshire now. If I were, I could drive one hour north to Maine and see a big piece of ice in a river. Maine is a very cold state, and there is usually ice in the rivers in winter, but this is a very special piece of ice. It is completely round, and it spins slowly in the middle of the river. You can find a photo if you look up "Westbrook, Maine news" on the Internet. It is about 90 meters wide. It is made up of many smaller pieces of ice that froze together. The more it went around, the rounder it became, and now it is a perfect circle.

perfect circle　完全な円　　round　丸い
be made up of 〜　〜でできている

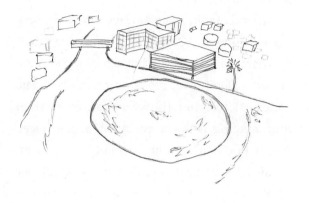

アメリカのメイン州はカナダのすぐ南にあるので，冬は北海道のように寒いです。隣のニューハンプシャー州に住んでいる姉の家が近いので，僕もこの神秘的な現象を見に行きたいと思いました。

3246

A friend of mine was amazed when she saw my cell phone. She saw the number 3246 on the mail icon at the bottom of my screen. "Wow! Don't you read your emails?" she asked. I told her that I am on more than four mailing lists. I get a lot of messages that I don't have time to read. She is on mailing lists, too. She doesn't read all her emails either, but she opens all of them. I looked at her phone, and sure enough, she hardly had any unopened emails. I decided to delete all my unread emails, but it takes a lot of time to get rid of all 3246.

unopened email　未読メール

 僕の携帯電話に表示されている未読メールの数を見たら驚くでしょう。このコメントを書いている今も2,006通あります。メーリングリストに参加していると毎日何十通も来るので，削除しないと，どんどん溜まります。

Yukizuri

Although it snows a lot in my hometown, gardeners have work in winter. It's called *yukizuri*. They do this to prevent the branches of trees from breaking from the weight of the snow. This is what the gardeners do: they stretch ropes from the top of a tree to the lower branches. Many ropes are used around the tree, so the tree takes the shape of a Japanese umbrella. When we see *yukizuri*, we feel that winter is approaching. By the way, I have *yukimi-shoji* in my house. They can be half-opened so that when we look outside, we can see the *yukizuri*.

(Written by a reader, Ichikawa Nobuhiro)

---

prevent A from 〜 ing　Aが〜するのを防ぐ　　　stretch　張る
take the shape of 〜　〜の形になる　　　approach　近づく
half-opened　半分開いた

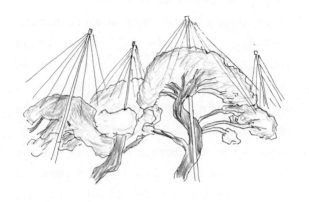

僕は雪吊りを写真では見たことはありますが，一度
雪の深い時に実際に見に行きたいと思っています。
この読者のように，暖かい部屋の中から雪見障子を
通して，ゆっくりと外の景色をながめるのはうらや
ましいですね。

From Number 72 to Number 1

The world was watching Osaka Naomi last Saturday. Could she win another grand slam after her win against Serena Williams last year at the U.S. Open? She played Petra Kvitova of the Czech Republic in the final game of the Australian Open in Melbourne. It was a very exciting game. Osaka won the first set, but then she lost the second set 5-7. In the third set she stayed ahead and finally won with a serve that Kvitova could not return. Osaka has won two grand slam tournaments in a row. She is now ranked the number 1 female tennis player of the world. One year ago, she was only number 72!

in a row　連続して　　be ranked 〜　〜にランク付けされている

 大坂なおみ選手が1年でどれだけ伸びたかはランキングで分かりますね。2018年1月は72位でしたが，全豪オープンで優勝した2019年1月には1位になりました。彼女の一番の武器はおそらく強烈なサーブでしょう。201キロを記録しています。返せるはずがありません！

How Many New Years?

Malaysia, where my husband and I live, is a nation of many races and religions. The Chinese New Year is coming soon, on February 5 and 6. The town is full of red decorations, and people are starting to celebrate. They have lunch or dinner with their family. Many Asian countries celebrate the Chinese New Year, but there are three other New Year celebrations in Malaysia. One is on January 1. Then, Muslims celebrate Hari Raya Puasa after Ramadan, the month of fasting. Finally, Hindus celebrate Deepavali in the autumn. I feel that Malaysia is a country where every culture is recognized.

(Written by a reader, Kojima Hiroe)

race 人種, 民族　　　religion 宗教

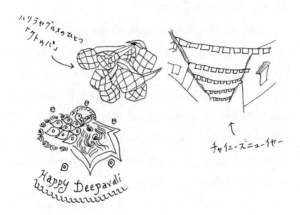

ハリラヤグルメのひとつ
「クトゥパッ」

チャイニーズニューイヤー

Happy Deepavali

マレーシアには新年のお祝いが4回もあるということですね。マレーシア人全員がすべての祭日を祝うとは思いませんが，それぞれのお祝いは楽しそうです。

Test Driving a Tesla

I had a chance to test drive a Tesla, an electric car which is made in America. If the battery is fully charged, the car can travel 300 km. This car costs at least 10 million yen. When I stepped on the accelerator, I felt like I was on a roller coaster because my body was pushed back into the leather seat. When another car came toward my car, I could see both cars on the control panel. This car has so many sensors that it can drive itself on the highway. I didn't try it, but another person did. He said that you have to hold onto the steering wheel or the car will give you a warning.

(Written by a reader, Goto Yasuhiro)

be fully charged　フル充電されている　　accelerator　アクセル
steering wheel　ハンドル　　warning　警告

Tesla
Model 3

テスラ社は 2003 年にアメリカで創立しました。従来のアメリカの自動車メーカーと違って，電気自動車をメインに作っています。2017 年から手が届く値段のセダンを販売し始めて，急速に人気を集めています。

Goodbye, Sakaiya Taichi

I was sad to hear of Sakaiya Taichi's death. I just discovered that that was his pen name. His real name was Ikeguchi Kotaro. He was a very talented person. He worked for the government and was the producer of the 1970 World Expo in Osaka, but I only knew him as a writer. I read two of his books, "The Twelve Men Who Made Japan" and "*Yudan*!" I especially enjoyed the first book. Sakaiya chose an interesting group of 12 men, from Shotoku Taishi to Matsushita Konosuke. He included Hikaru Genji even though the man is a character in a book, not a real person.

talented　才能のある　　the World Expo　万国博覧会，万博
character　登場人物

 堺屋太一さんを知ったのは「日本を創った 12 人」という本でした。もともと歴史が好きな僕ですが，選ばれた 12 人が今の日本人の考え方にどのような影響を与えたのかという内容はとても興味深いです。この本はおすすめです。

Waitresses or Tablets?

Have you ever been to a restaurant where a computer takes your order? I went to one where they gave us a tablet. We were able to choose between several different languages just by pressing a button. That was the easy part. When we tried to order, however, it was difficult to navigate. I touched the name of the food, but nothing happened. Then my friend tried. We kept on touching the screen until we touched the price. Then a new screen came up, and we were able to place our order. The food and drinks came very quickly, but my friend and I agreed that we prefer to talk to people.

take one's order　注文を取る　　place one's order　注文する

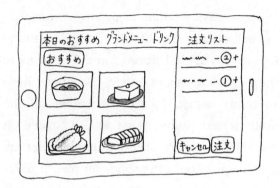

あるレストランでは，タブレットが渡されて，店員がいなくても注文できる仕組みになっていました。最近は外国人客が増えたため，多言語に対応しているデジタルメニューは便利だと思います。でも，料理を運んできた店員さんと話をしたら，やっぱり人間と話す方がいいなと思いました。

The Shuffle Feature on My Phone

These days I listen to my own music on my cell phone. I only recently added all my CDs to my digital library, and I have more than 3,000 pieces of music. Because I have so many songs, I can't remember all the albums that I have. Last week I turned on the shuffle feature on my phone and let my music app choose the songs for me. It plays one song and then chooses the next from a different album. It's exciting because I don't know what will come next. At the same time, it can be a little strange. Yesterday I listened to R&B, then jazz, then a rock song, and finally an aria from an opera.

shuffle feature　シャッフル（ランダムに再生する）機能
add　加える

数十年間集めてきた CD なので，若いころに好き
だったロックもあれば，クラシックもあります。「こ
んな曲もあったなあ」と久しぶりに聞く曲がたくさ
んあります。いつ何が再生されるかまったく分かり
ませんが，それが面白いです。

Spring on the Way?

Is spring on its way? I think so. It was very warm yesterday, but that is not the only reason. The plum trees in Nagoya have started to bloom. They say that plum blossoms signal the beginning of spring. You can tell a plum tree from a cherry tree because plum trees are not as tall. They don't grow along the sides of streets or along rivers, so they don't make a strong impression from a distance. One plum tree stands alone at the entrance to the local shrine near my apartment. When I get near, I can see the little round white blossoms on the branches. Each little flower is beautiful.

plum （ここでは）ウメ　　bloom　花が咲く
tell A from B　AとBを区別する　　impression　印象
shrine　神社

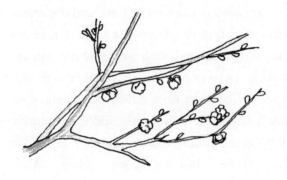

桜は公園や道端に並んで咲いているのがとても美しいですが，梅は違います。梅園もありますが，僕は1本の梅の木を見つけてその花を1つ1つ見る方が好きです。

Great Parking Job!

I am always amazed at how well Japanese drivers can park. There are some houses in my neighborhood with very narrow garage doors. Drivers carefully back their cars into the garage with only a few centimeters on each side, but they never make a mistake. Why am I talking about parking? Because last Friday, Japan's space agency, JAXA, showed the world that it could do something even harder. It landed Hayabusa 2 on the small, rocky Ryugu asteroid. Hayabusa 2 is collecting samples and will come back to Earth in 2020. Then we can learn more about the beginning of the universe!

narrow 狭い   JAXA 宇宙航空研究開発機構
asteroid 小惑星   the universe 宇宙

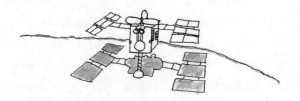

細い道で運転する日本人，ドアを開ける隙間がない
くらい狭いガレージに車を入れる日本人，どちらも
高い運転技術を持っています。宇宙においてもこの
技術が活かされているように思います。

Teaching Japanese Culture

Some students from my university are in Australia now. They are spending their days at kindergartens and primary schools in the Melbourne area. It is a great experience for them. Not only can they watch the Australian teachers teach; they also have a chance to teach Japanese culture. Some have chosen Japanese games, and some have chosen crafts. One student is going to teach the children how to make their own *kendama* using a paper cup, string, and a ball of aluminum foil. They will give the younger children ready-made paper cup *kendama*, but the older ones will make them themselves.

primary school　小学校　　craft　工作
aluminum foil　アルミホイル

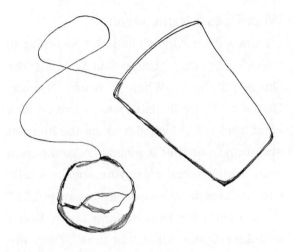

 子どもは遊びを通じて学ぶと考えられていますが，
日本人大学生も遊びながら英語を使うと習得できる
のではないでしょうか。少なくとも必要に迫られて
「使わなきゃ！」という気になるでしょう。

What Does a Name Mean?

I knew that "John" had the meaning of "toilet" and that "Uncle Sam" meant the United States. When I heard "Hooray Henry" from my British friend, I had no idea what it meant. I looked it up on the Internet and found out that it means "A young man from a high social class who speaks loudly and behaves in a noticeable way in public." No wonder! We were talking about Brexit and the referendum at that time. There are many nouns and idioms that use people's names. I think that's really interesting, by George!

(Written by a reader, Watanabe Seiko)

behave in a noticeable way　目立った行動をする
No wonder!　なるほど！　　referendum　国民投票
By George!　本当に！

 なぜ人の名前が使われているのでしょうか？ イギリスで水洗トイレを初めて考案したのが John という人でした。アメリカでは，Samuel という人が約200年前に兵士たちに肉を提供していました。その肉の樽には U.S. と書かれていて，United States を表していましたが，誰かが Uncle Sam の略だと言った冗談が広まり，Uncle Sam は最終的に合衆国を象徴するキャラクターとなりました。

Lion Paparazzi

We went on a photo safari at Murchison Falls National Park in northwestern Uganda. We got up early and went out to look for animals before sunrise. The first animal we saw was an antelope. Then we saw warthogs. After the sun came up, we passed giraffes, elephants and a hyena. There were amazing birds everywhere! Down by the Nile, some hippos were swimming, but we couldn't find any lions. We got an earlier start the next day. This time our guide found a group of lions, all females. We were joined by another van and followed them for 30 minutes, taking photos.

antelope　レイヨウ，アンテロープ　　warthog　イボイノシシ
hippo (hippopotamus の略)　カバ

 ライオンを見たくてフォトサファリに来る人はたく さんいますが，僕自身はライオンにはこだわりませ ん。どの野生動物を見ても感動していました。でも， 2日目に暗闇の中，道で寝ているハイエナやライオ ンを見つけたのはとても興奮しました。皆の夢がか なって良かったです！

Living Together in Peace

Ugandans are very religious. Most are Christian, but about 15-20% believe in Islam. In some countries, these two religions don't get along, but in Uganda people of both religions show respect for each other's beliefs. For example, in the restaurant at our hotel in Kampala, they don't serve pork because believers in Islam do not eat it. People who want pork go to special restaurants for it. While we were driving through the countryside, we saw small churches and mosques in the same villages. People of both religions live side by side in peace.

religious　信心深い　　belief　信仰

今の世の中では，イスラム教とキリスト教が敵対関係に陥りがちですが，ウガンダでは大きな問題もなく共存しています。首都のカンパラ市では，ある丘の上に教会があれば，他の丘の上には大きなモスクがあります。ホテルでは，イスラム教徒に配慮して，イスラム教で禁じられている豚肉を使ったメニューはありません。

Use Your English!

One boy in Okayama can speak English very well. He has been learning English since he was a baby. By the time he was four years old, he could speak in sentences. His mother took him to Korakuen in Okayama so that he could speak to the foreign visitors there. He is 10 or 11 years old now, and he has become a volunteer guide at the garden! He walks around the garden wearing a vest that says, "I am TAKUTO! Please feel free to talk to me in English!" He knows a lot about the garden and can even explain what *kibidango* is! If you want to learn how to speak, do what he does. Use your English!

in sentences 文で   explain 説明する

 10歳くらいの男の子がやってきて，「後楽園を英語で案内しましょうか？」と流暢な英語で外国人観光客に話しかけます。YouTube で検索すると川上拓土くんの活動ぶりを見られます。この子の積極性はすごいですね。大きくなったらきっと国連大使になれます！

Swallowed by a Whale!

Every year a lot of sardines (small fish) swim along the coast of South Africa. They are followed by predators: penguins, dolphins, sharks and whales. These predators swim around the sardines so that sardines make a ball in the water. Then they attack and eat the sardines. Last month, a diver wanted to get pictures of the sardines close up, so he jumped from his boat into the middle of the sardine ball. All of a sudden, it got dark around him. A whale had come up from below and swallowed him by accident. Whales cannot eat people, so it let him go. He was safe, but he was very surprised!

---

swallow　飲み込む　　sardine　イワシ
predator　天敵，捕食動物　　all of a sudden　突然に
by accident　偶然

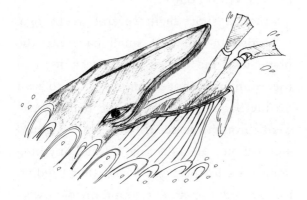

無数のイワシの群れを狙って、南アフリカの沖に魚，
クジラ，イルカ，サメ，海鳥などがやって来ます。
その水中風景を撮りたくて海に潜った写真家が，ク
ジラの口からお尻を出した状態で撮影の対象になっ
てしまいました。他の写真家がその姿をバッチリ撮
影しました。

Found, Then Lost

I took a short flight several weeks ago. I decided to take my small bag onto the plane with me rather than check it in at the counter because I didn't want to wait for my bag when I got off the plane. As I went through the security check, the guard stopped me. He asked me if I had anything dangerous in the bag. I said that I didn't. He X-rayed it again and found my old Swiss army knife at the bottom of the bag. I'd been looking for it for almost a year, but I had never checked inside the Boston bag. I was happy to see it, but I couldn't take it on the flight. They took it away from me.

security check　保安検査場　　X-ray　X線で調べる
check　確認する　　take A away from 〜　Aを〜から取り上げる

知らないうちにスイスアーミーナイフがボストン
バッグの底に潜んでいました。ずっと探していたの
に，やっと出てきたと思ったら，取り上げられてし
まいました。この日はツイてなかったです。

There Will Never Be Another Ichiro

Last Thursday, Ichiro retired from professional baseball. If you have never seen him play, look at his best moments on YouTube. He is one of the greatest players in baseball history. He broke records when he played in Japan, and then he went over to the Major Leagues in 2001 and broke more records. He could hit any ball. In one year, he got 262 hits, which is still a record. He had more than 200 hits every season for his first 10 years with the Mariners. He was a great outfielder with an unbelievable throwing arm, and he was great at stealing bases, too. There will never be another Ichiro!

retire 引退する   outfielder 外野手
unbelievable 信じられないほどすばらしい
throwing arm 強肩   steal bases 盗塁する

イチロー選手は日本でもアメリカでも最高の選手でした。MLB に所属してから 10 年連続で 200 以上のヒットを打った選手は他にいません。打つことができても，速く走れないと一塁に間に合わないので，彼の総合力があってこそできたことでしょう。

True Friendship

In 2011, an old man on a small island near Rio de Janeiro, Brazil, found a penguin. It was covered in oil and was dying. Mr. de Souza took it home and spent many days cleaning and feeding it. He gave it a name, Dindim. When Dindim was strong enough to swim, the man took him back to another island and let him go. But the penguin came back and stayed with de Souza for months. Dindim finally left in February. Then, in June, de Souza heard Dindim calling outside the house. He was back again! He comes back every year and spends more than half of the year with de Souza. What a friendship!

friendship 友情
be covered in 〜 〜で覆われている，〜まみれである
feed 餌を与える

ペンギンが毎年島に戻っておじいさんに会いに来る
なんて昔話の恩返しのようですね。ディンディムは
他の人には触らせませんが、デ・ソウザさんだけは
ディンディムを持ち上げて膝の上に乗せることがで
きるそうです。

Where Do I Get Off?

I went to a university for a conference last month. I had to leave early so I was the only one on the elevator. I pushed the first floor button, and the elevator went down. When the doors opened, I knew I was on the wrong floor. Maybe the exit was on the second floor. I went up, but that was the wrong floor, too. I went up to the third floor, but I still couldn't find out how to leave the building. Finally, the elevator went back up to the fifth floor, and some other people got on. They told me that I had to push "G" and go to the ground floor. This university uses the British system!

exit　出口
ground floor　（イギリスでは）1階（アメリカでは 1 階は first floor）

日本ではアメリカのように1階は「1」と表示するのが普通です。なぜ名古屋の某大学では階の呼び方が日本風ではなくイギリス風なのか分かりませんが，きっと大学の創立者がイギリス崇拝者なのだと思います。

School Bag Drone

Children in Japan have to carry a lot of heavy books to school. One school bag maker wants to help them with a school bag drone. This drone can carry a bag on a special hook. Children turn on the drone using a cell phone app, and the drone lifts the school bag up in the air. Then it follows the children to school. It is easy to use because of AI. The drone automatically stays one meter behind the children. Give your child a break! Go to 4fools.co.jp today to order this drone at a special one-day only discount.

app アプリ   automatically 自動的に   order 注文する

 今日は何の日ですか？　エイプリルフールですよ！人間についていくドローンはありますが，日本の小学生が背負っている重いランドセルを持ち上げるほどの家庭用ドローンは，まだ開発されていないと思います。

The First and the Last

Toho was the first high school in the Heisei Era to win the National High School Baseball Invitational Tournament. That was in 1989. Now, 30 years later, the team is strong again. They went into this year's tournament with the goal of winning it. Yesterday was the final game. They played against Narashino High School. The star of Toho was Ishikawa Takaya. He pitched for Toho and didn't give up a run. Not only that, but he hit two home runs, and Toho became the last high school in the Heisei Era to win the spring baseball tournament.

the National High School Baseball Invitational Tournament　選抜高等学校野球大会(春の甲子園)
final game　決勝戦　　give up a run　1点を許す

 平成元年に春の甲子園で優勝した東邦高校が，平成
最後の年に30年ぶりに優勝しました。小説に出て
くるような奇跡的な話です。石川昂弥選手は投手と
してもホームランバッターとしても大活躍でした。
ちなみに彼は卒業後，中日ドラゴンズに入ることが
決まりました。

Why Use *Hiragana*?

Yesterday there were elections all over Japan. People in Nagoya chose the members of the Nagoya City Council. I was happy because the sound trucks were finally silent. No one went around yesterday shouting the name of their candidate. During the election, I saw the names of some candidates on the sound trucks. Some of the first names were written in *hiragana*. I understand why they use *hiragana*. First names can be difficult to read. This time, however, I noticed some family names in *hiragana*. I was surprised because family names are usually easy to read. Why did they use *hiragana*?

election　選挙　　city council　市議会
sound truck　（ここでは)選挙カー　　candidate　候補者

アメリカの選挙では，表に候補者名が載っていて印をつけるだけで投票できますが，日本の場合は候補者の名前を自筆で記入することになっています。字を間違えると票が無効になるおそれがあるから，誰でも間違えずに書けるひらがななら安全という理由でひらがなにしているのでしょうか？

Do You Want to Be a Ninja?

A company that puts on ninja shows in Iga City is looking for young people to work for them. They are looking for people who love ninja and can work hard. They will give you an interview and a practical test. If you get the job, you will start as an apprentice. You will learn how to throw ninja stars, fight with swords, and use blow darts. Last year, fake news on SNS said that they were hiring ninja for 10,000,000 yen a year. This year, they are hiring, but first-year apprentices will only get 150,000-180,000 yen a month. Do you want to be a ninja?

apprentice 見習い　　ninja star 手裏剣　　blow dart 吹き矢
hire 雇う

2018年のフェイクニュースだった「伊賀市で忍者大募集！」は，翌年に実話になりました。ただし，最初は見習いということで給料はそんなによくありません。もう少し若ければ僕も応募したかもしれません。

Have You Seen a 2,000-yen Bill Recently?

The government says that there will be new faces on the 10,000-yen bill, the 5,000-yen bill, and the 1,000-yen bill in 2024. When I first came to Japan, I remember seeing Shotoku Taishi and Ito Hirobumi. Then came Fukuzawa Yukichi, Nitobe Inazo, and Natsume Soseki. There are two more new faces now. American money is different. George Washington has been on the $1 bill since I was born. So have Lincoln ($5), Hamilton ($10), and Jackson ($20). There is one similarity between Japanese money and American money, however. Americans seldom use the $2 bill, and I hardly ever see a 2,000-yen bill.

bill　紙幣
Hamilton　（アレクサンダー・）ハミルトン，アメリカの初代財務長官
Jackson　（アンドリュー・）ジャクソン，アメリカの第７代大統領
similarity　類似点，共通点

 二千円札も2ドル札もめったに見ません。二千円札は2000年に沖縄サミットを記念してできたものですが，普及していません。2ドル札の歴史はもっと長いですが，やはり普及しませんでした。1と5の間に2は要らなさそうですね。

Hay Fever

Last week I asked a class of adults which season they liked the best. I like spring because it gets warmer every day, and there are many flowering plants. Not everyone agreed with me. Some people dislike spring because they have hay fever. They sneeze and cough all day long. My wife is one of those unlucky people. Her hay fever comes from Japanese cedars. It started in February this year, and she says that it won't go away until after Golden Week. Is there any place where people don't have hay fever? I hear that Okinawa is a good place to go. I think it is because there are few cedars there.

hay fever　花粉症　　sneeze　くしゃみをする　　cough　咳をする
Japanese cedar　スギ

「春が好きじゃない」という発言に最初は驚きましたが，花粉症で悩まされる人にとっては大変な季節ですね。花粉症は昔はなかったのでしょうか？　もし，松尾芭蕉が花粉症に悩まされていたら，「春くしゃみ　杉ひのきから　金の雨」のような俳句を書いたかも？

A Cherry Blossom Viewing Trip

Last week, my husband and I took a trip to Kyoto. The downtown area was crowded with foreigners. Almost all the women who were walking along the street in kimono were Chinese. The cherry blossoms were at their best during our stay. I have never seen such wonderful cherry blossoms in my life. I especially love weeping cherry trees. I think that those trees go well with old temples. The branches have many cherry blossoms, but those petals fall gracefully after just one or two weeks. No wonder many foreigners want to come to Japan to see cherry blossoms.

(Written by a reader, Bando Shinko)

weeping cherry tree　シダレザクラ　　petal　花びら

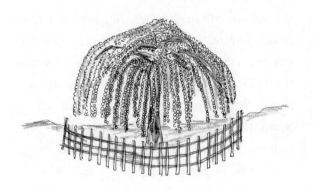

この読者のように，僕も桜が満開の京都を一度は訪れてみたいです。寺の設計者は自然の美しさを理解していて，建物に合うような庭を作ったのでしょう。暖かい春の日に，銀閣寺の近くにある「哲学の道」を歩きながら桜を見ると気持ちが良いでしょう。

Anything Is Possible

Iwamoto Mitsuhiro has become the first blind person to sail across the Pacific Ocean. He piloted his 12-meter yacht while his American navigator, Doug Smith, guided him. This wasn't his first try. In 2013, Iwamoto left from Fukushima Prefecture, but his boat was hit by a whale and sank. This time he went the other way. He left San Diego on Feb. 24 and arrived at Iwaki, Fukushima Prefecture, on April 20. It took him and Smith almost two months to sail 14,000 kilometers. Why did he do it? He wanted to show the world that "anything is possible when people come together."

blind　目の不自由な　　navigator　航海士
come together　協力する

岩本光弘さんがアメリカ人の航海士と一緒にヨットで太平洋を横断したことは，最高の冒険だと思います。穏やかな日はともかく，海が荒れている時に甲板で足をすべらせて命を落としそうになるなどの危険がたくさんあったに違いありません。

The Longest Golden Week

Welcome to the new Reiwa Era! Yesterday was the end of the longest Golden Week in the history of Japan. Many workers had 10 days off in a row, from April 27 to May 6. About 25,000,000 people were traveling during the holidays. Many people were traveling abroad, and the most popular foreign destinations were China and Korea. There were many people traveling around Japan too. The traffic jams were bad, but some of the trains were not as crowded. Because the holidays were longer, everyone didn't have to return at the same time.

destination　目的地, 行き先　　traffic jam　交通渋滞

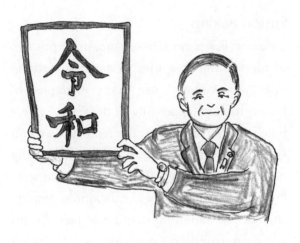

 今回の即位は突然の崩御のためではなく，計画に基づいたものだったので，多くの会社員には，令和の始まりだったゴールデンウィークで 10 日間の休みがありました。普段なかなか長く休めない人にとってはチャンスでした。

Fusion Baking

Fusion is a great idea. It means to put two or more things together to make something new. In Japan, I see many examples of fusion in food, especially in desserts. Chefs take a dessert from another food culture and add Japanese flavors to make something new. On Saturday, I had a barbecue with my daughter and her husband's family. One of the children is quite a baker, and she made a chiffon cake for us. It wasn't the usual chiffon cake. It was a *sakura*-flavored cake. She made it with cherry blossoms that she had picked and salted at the beginning of April. It was sweet, salty, and delicious!

salt　塩漬けにする

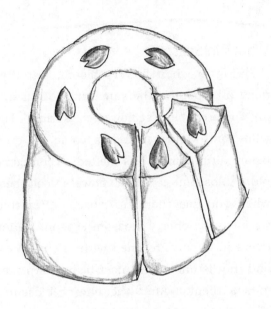

抹茶味のお菓子は流行していますが，桜を使った洋菓子は抹茶に比べて少ないように思います。高校１年生が自分で塩漬けにした桜の花びらを使って，桜のシフォンケーキを作る想像力と実践力がすごいと思います。一流のパティシエになれるといいですね！

What's in Season?

Spring is when flowers bloom, but they don't all bloom at the same time. Daffodils are some of the first flowers of spring. The white and yellow trumpets come up even before all the snow has melted. Then come plum blossoms. These flowers look best when you see them up close. After that we have the cherry blossom season. Many rivers in Japan are lined with cherry trees, and that is one of the most beautiful places to see them. After the cherry blossoms come the azaleas which look like little pink and purple trumpets. What is in season now? I think roses are.

daffodil　スイセン　　up close　近くで　　azalea　ツツジ

色の少ない冬から鮮やかな花が咲く春になると，心も明るくなります。僕の住んでいる名古屋の冬はそれほど長くはありませんが，北海道の冬は長く続きます。そのため，北海道の人たちは春に対する期待が大きいのでしょう。

Troutani

Ohtani Shohei started playing with the L.A. Angels again. He was out of the game for over half a year after having Tommy John surgery on his right elbow last October. He returned two weeks ago and has just hit his second home run this season. The Angels now have a great lineup. Mike Trout is one of the best hitters in MLB now. He bats second, and Ohtani bats third. Together, they are helping the Angels to win again. The two hitters are such a good pair that some fans have started calling them Troutani (Trout + Ohtani). Go, Troutani!

surgery　手術　　lineup　打順

トラウト選手と大谷選手は，日本のかつての名選手の長嶋茂雄さんと王貞治さんのようになるのでしょうか？　大谷選手が手術を受けるために休んでもファンの熱は冷めませんでした。この大物選手が早く打者だけではなく，投手としても活躍できるようになってほしいですね。

Not Prince Shotoku

Shotoku Taishi is one of the most important leaders in Japanese history. There are many stories showing how great he was. According to Nihon Shoki, he could understand 10 people speaking to him at the same time. The other day, I turned on my computer while I was listening to my wife. I started to read an email while she was speaking. In the middle of the email, she finished what she was saying. I knew that I should say something, but I hadn't been listening to her. I apologized and said, "What did you say?" My wife said jokingly, "I'm disappointed. I thought you were Prince Shotoku."

apologize　謝る

 僕が聖徳太子のように複数の話を同時に聞くのはありえないですね。1人の話でさえ聞くのは難しいので，10人はとても無理です。複数のことを同時に行うマルチタスキングは女性が向いていて，男性はあまり向いていないと言われていますが，聖徳太子の例をみればそうとは限りません。

May Sickness

In Japan, new jobs and the new school year start in April. After Golden Week, some students and new employees feel depressed. They lose their energy and their interest in things, and they stop coming to school or work. This is called *gogatsu-byo* or "May sickness." I used to think it was peculiarly Japanese. Then I found out that students in other countries have the same problem a month after they enter university. This feeling can happen to people after a long vacation, too. It is called "post-vacation blues." Maybe "May sickness" is so bad in Japan because it comes after Golden Week.

new employee　新入社員　　depressed　落ち込んだ
peculiarly　特有に

 僕は五月病を経験したことはありませんが，新しい仕事が始まる前に落ち着かなくなり，仕事がうまくできるか悩むことはあります。五月病は似たような気持ちなのでしょう。しばらく我慢しても結局慣れないと，仕事や学校に行けなくなるのかもしれません。

Hokkaido Is Hot!

Is it hot enough for you? I can't believe that it's hotter in Hokkaido than here in Nagoya. In fact, on Sunday the temperature reached 39.5 degrees in Saroma in the north of Hokkaido. The usual May temperatures there range from 4-16 degrees. Even the summer temperatures usually only get up to 25 degrees. The poor people who live there! They have probably never felt anything like that before, and I'm sure that no one has an air conditioner. How did they survive the heat? In heat like that, it's best to stay inside, drink a lot of liquids, and eat salt candy.

range from A to B　A から B に及ぶ
poor people　かわいそうな人々　　survive　耐える

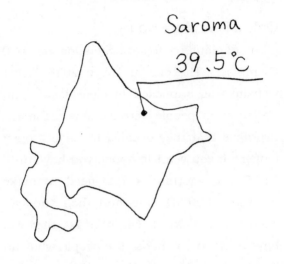

Saroma
39.5℃

名古屋に住む人たちにとって，夏の気温が 30 度後半に達することは日常茶飯事ですが，もともと涼しいところで育った人にとって，この暑さは未知の世界ですね。異常気象は全世界で起こりえるようになっていて，本当に気になりますね。

Only a Few More Hours!

You can still try to get tickets for the 2020 Olympics! The official Tokyo 2020 Ticket website was supposed to close last night, but so many people were using it in the last two days that they decided to leave it open longer. If you want to apply, you have until 11:59 this morning. You need to make a Tokyo 2020 ID first, and then you can choose your tickets. On June 20, they will have a lottery to choose the people who can buy tickets. Hurry! You only have a few more hours. Remember that only people who live in Japan can apply.

be supposed to 〜　〜することになっている　　apply　申し込む
lottery　くじ引き

このようなチケット販売は，なぜこんなに複雑になったのでしょうか？　僕の想像では，たくさんのチケットが不正に売りさばかれないように気を付けているからでしょう。多少めんどうでも仕方がないことです。

June 3, 2019

How to Kill an Hour

I went to a language teaching conference in Tokyo over the weekend. I've known some of the teachers for more than 15 years. Of course, we talk about teaching, but the conference is also like a reunion, a chance to see old friends. Last night I had a long talk with one teacher. We had dinner, but I still had a couple of hours before my bus left. We didn't feel like coffee. Can you guess where we spent an hour talking? On the Yamanote Line. We started at Harajuku and took the train all the way around Tokyo! When we got back to Shinjuku, we said goodbye and I went on to Tokyo Station.

kill an hour　1 時間つぶす　　reunion　同窓会

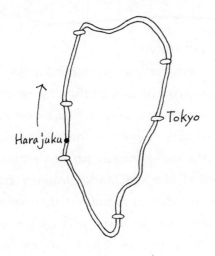

Harajuku

Tokyo

←— Yamanote Line

ずっと山手線を一周したいと思っていましたが，
やっと夢がかないました。かなったと言っても友達
と話し込んでいたため，電車の外をほとんど見よう
としませんでした。結局夜の 10 時ごろに友達が新
宿駅で降りて，僕はそのまま東京駅まで行きました。
その後，僕は夜行バスに乗って帰りました。

Go-karts in Tokyo

While I was walking to Harajuku Station with a couple of friends on Sunday evening, we saw something unusual. There were four or five go-karts stopped at the traffic lights. The drivers were dressed up in costumes. They looked like the Mario Brothers from a Nintendo game. I found out that several companies rent go-karts and guide you around the streets of Tokyo. If you have a driver's license, you can rent one. There are several tours, some going to Akihabara, Tokyo Skytree, and even across the Rainbow Bridge to Odaiba. What a way to see Tokyo!

unusual　普通でない

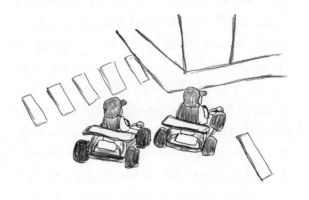

東京でゴーカートを乗り回すことはファンタジー映画の1シーンのようですが，それは現実になりました。東京のゴーカートツアーが外国の観光客の間で大人気です。僕はゴーカートに乗ってみたいとは思いますが，車道ではなくサーキットを回りたいと思います。

Sani Brown Sets a New Japanese Record

On June 7, Sani Brown set a new Japanese record for the men's 100-meter sprint at the NCAA Track & Field Championships in Austin, Texas. The record had been held by Kiryu Yoshihide since 2017 when Kiryu set a Japanese record of 9.98 seconds. Last Friday, Sani Brown ran for the University of Florida where he is studying. He ran 100 meters in 9.97 seconds, beating Kiryu's record by 0.01 seconds. He came in third after Divine Oduduru of Nigeria and Craven Gillespie of the U.S.A. Oduduru came in first, Gillespie second, and Sani Brown third in the 200-meter race, too.

set a record　記録を樹立する
the NCAA Track & Field Championships　全米大学体育協会の陸上競技選手権大会，陸上の全米大学選手権

陸上の短距離レースは，秒で測りきれません。サニブラウン選手が桐生選手の日本記録を破ったのはたった 0.01 秒差です。世界記録はウサイン・ボルト選手が 2009 年に 9.58 秒をマークして以来，誰も破っていません。サニブラウン選手の今回の記録とは 0.39 秒差です。

Toast for Breakfast

My husband and I have toast for breakfast. I like thinly sliced toast, but my husband prefers thick toast. I buy a 5-slice pack for him and an 8-slice pack for myself. According to a major baking company, the 6-slice pack is the No.1 seller in Kanto, while in Kansai, the 5-slice pack tops the list. It means that Kansai people like thicker bread, and in Kanto, they prefer thinner slices. They say it comes from the different food culture of the two areas. Kansai people have a taste for soft, spongy food like *okonomiyaki*. Kanto people have a *senbei* culture. They like crisp, crunchy food.

(Written by a reader, Terumoto Miwako)

top the list　1 位を占める　　have a taste for ～　～を好む
spongy　やわらかい，フワフワした　　crisp　カリッとした
crunchy　サクサクした

関東の人は納豆が好きで，関西の人は好きではない
という食文化の違いを聞いたことがありますが，好
む食感の違いについては初耳でした。名古屋は関東
と関西の間に挟まれていますが，名古屋の味はとて
も濃いとされています。これもまた違う食文化です
ね。

It's Winter in Australia

I have been living in Australia since January as a study abroad student. I'm in the Southern Hemisphere now, which means it's winter. We don't really have rain in summer, but there is a lot of rain in winter. It isn't humid, but it is freezing! When I saw pictures of my friends wearing sleeveless shirts, it made me jealous and sad. I think the cold weather makes us a little sad compared to warm weather. I don't like the rainy season in Japan, so I'm glad that I don't need to feel uncomfortable this year. But I'm little worried about the crops in Japan. Farmers can't raise crops without rain.

(Written by a reader, Nakashima Saki)

the Southern Hemisphere 南半球　　sleeveless 袖なしの
raise crops 農作物を作る

 南半球と北半球の季節は正反対ですね。日本が寒くなると，逆にオーストラリアが暑くなります。この読者はきっと日本が雨不足という情報を聞いて心配していたのでしょうが，数か月後に日本は涼しくなり，オーストラリアでは猛暑によって記録的な山火事が発生しました。

Hachimura Rui Goes to the NBA

Hachimura Rui has been a great basketball player since high school. He was the star of the Meisei High School team which won the All-Japan High School Tournament three times. Then he went to Gonzaga University because it has one of the best basketball teams in America. At first, he could speak very little English and couldn't understand the coach. He worked hard on his English and his basketball, and he was selected as WCC Player of the Year. He will leave his university to join the Washington Wizards in the NBA's next season. The Wizards want him because he is a good two-way player.

(the) WCC　全米大学体育協会の西部地区 (= the West Coast Conference)
two-way player　攻撃と守備を両方できる選手

八村塁選手は英語を一生懸命に勉強し，SAT（アメリカ式センター試験）のスコアを伸ばしてゴンザガ大学に入学しました。大学で3年間プレーしてから，ワシントン・ウィザーズのドラフト1巡目指名を受けて，プロ入りを果たしました。

Studying for a Junior High School Test

I was helping my granddaughter with her English homework last weekend. This is her first year of junior high school, and she has a lot of tests this week. I saw how she studied. She took words from her textbook and wrote each down about 10 times. That's one way to learn English spelling. Then she wanted to know the meaning of each word in Japanese. That works for nouns like "friend" and "baseball," but I was surprised when she asked how to translate "thank" and "welcome." I told her that we seldom use these words alone. We usually use them in phrases such as "Thank you" and "You're welcome."

granddaughter　孫娘　　phrase　フレーズ

Thank + you

You're + welcome

孫娘の英単語の覚え方は，日本語にたとえると「ど
ういたしまして」の「どう」を10回書いて，「いたし
まして」を10回書いてからその2つをくっつけるよ
うなやり方です。意味を考えて勉強しているように
は思えません。"You're welcome"は1つのフレーズ
で，"Thank you"という感謝表現に対する決まり文
句ですね。

Learn How to Use "It"

If you look at the 10 most common words in the English language, you will find two words that do not exist in Japanese: "a" and "the." There is no way to translate them, so there is no way to understand them in Japanese. You have to learn how to use them in English sentences. And what about the word "it"? Some teachers translate it as "*sore*," but how often do Japanese speakers use the word "*sore*"? Not very often. How often is "it" used in English? All the time! It is one of the most common words in English. You can't translate "it." You just have to learn how to use it.

"It" ≠ それ

英和辞典を作る先生方は，it を調べたい学習者のために適切な定義を載せる義務を感じているに違いありません。日本語では主語を省略する傾向があるので，it はほとんどの場合省略されます。it を一語で表そうとすると，結局「それ」になります。

An Email from Wikipedia

I got an email from Wikipedia yesterday. Wikipedia is an online encyclopedia that is written by volunteers. Some people don't think you can trust the information, but I think it is one of the best ways to find out about things you don't know. It has information about almost anything. It is also a great tool for translators. If you want to know the name of an animal in another language, go to the Wikipedia page in your own language. Then go to the English (or another language) page. You'll learn how it is said and written. Wikipedia sent me an email asking for money, and I was happy to give them some.

encyclopedia　百科事典　　trust　信用する　　translator　翻訳者

WIKIPEDIA
The Free Encyclopedia

English
5964000+articles

Español
1554000+articulos

Русский
1576000+статей

Italiano
1562000+voci

Português
1014000+artigos

日本語
1175000+記事

Deutsch
2361000+Artikel

Français
2152000+articles

中文
1080000+條目

Polski
1367000+haset

珍しい生きものや現在話題になっている人たちは辞書に載っていません。日本語のウィキペディアで検索してから英語のページに切り替えると英語表記が簡単に見つかります。「じゃれマガ」を書くのにウィキペディアは欠かせません。

Petit-jiman

Do you have a *"petit-jiman"*? It is something that you are proud of, but it should be something funny and light, nothing seriously achieved or accomplished. My 25-year-old son is in Kagoshima now on a training program, and he was interviewed by a TV program in the downtown area. He was asked about his *petit-jiman* and replied that he'd gotten pretty good scores in school and had won the lottery when he visited Las Vegas. The TV crew did not like either of those answers, but they were happy when he said, "My face looks like the face of the main character in the movie 'Avatar'!"

(Written by a reader, Watanabe Seiko)

achieve　達成する　　accomplish　成し遂げる　　lottery　宝くじ

「プチ」というフランス語を「自慢」という日本語にくっつけたこの表現は僕にとって初耳でしたが，意味はよく分かりました。「英語ではどう言うの？」と聞かれたら困りますが，たぶん little things that you can brag about でしょうか？

Who Can Eat the Most Hot Dogs?

What do people in New York City do on the Fourth of July? Some of them go down to Coney Island, one of New York City's oldest beaches. It's a good time to go swimming, but many stop to see Nathan's Famous Hot Dog Eating Contest. Since 2011, there has been a separate contest for men and women. Each contest has about 20 contestants who try to eat the largest number of hot dogs in 10 minutes. Sonya Thomas holds the record for women: 45 hot dogs. Joey Chestnut holds the record for men: 74 hot dogs. This year's winners were Joey Chestnut and Miki Sudo, but neither of them broke previous records.

separate　別々の　　contestant　出場者
hold the record　記録を保持する　　previous　以前の

10分で74本だと，1分で7本以上のホットドッグを食べるペースですね。小林尊さんが2001年のコンテストに登場してから，記録が一気に20本台から50本台になりました。そのコツは分かりませんが，普通の人間にできるはずはないと思います。

A Second Chance

Tanaka Masahiro, known by his nickname Ma-kun in Japan, played on the American League team in the 2019 MLB All-Star Game on Tuesday, July 9. It wasn't the first time that he was chosen for an MLB All-Star Game. He was chosen in 2014 when he was a rookie with the New York Yankees. At that time, he had an elbow injury and could not play. This was his second chance, and he did a great job. He pitched the second inning of the All-Star Game and didn't give up any runs. The American League went on to win 4-3, and Tanaka was the winning pitcher.

elbow injury　ひじのけが　　give up a run　（1）点を許す

 大谷翔平選手が大リーグに移籍した後，日本の新聞は田中将大投手をあまり取り上げていませんでしたが，ヤンキースの主力ピッチャーとしてずっと活躍しています。今回は，2014年のオールスターゲームに選ばれた時にプレーできなかったことへのリベンジでしたね。

Four Leaves

The first live concert I ever went to was Four Leaves, a 4-man idol group from Johnny & Associates. I was an emotional junior high school student. I cried listening to their LP records and smiled at their posters in my room. I saw them in my hometown. I rushed to the JR station after the concert and was lucky enough to give a small key chain to my favorite singer. The members came to the window and waved goodbye to the fans. Then I saw the key chain hanging from the waist of my favorite singer's jeans. Just last week Johnny Kitagawa, the founder of Johnny & Associates, died at the age of 87.

(Written by a reader, Watanabe Seiko)

emotional　感情的な　　LP record　LP 盤，レコード
rush　駆けつける　　founder　創立者

この読者の10代のころの話でしょうが，最近の AKBや韓流歌手の追っかけをやっている人を見ると，熱狂的になるのに年齢は関係なさそうです。この読者の経験は一生忘れられないでしょう。

A Noisy Day

Is the rainy season over in Nagoya? I don't know if the weather forecasters have said that it is, but the weather will be hot and sunny for the next few days. This morning, for the first time this year, I can hear cicadas from my apartment. Thousands of them live at the campus of the university across the street. When they start singing all at once, I know that the rainy season is over. Actually, I was surprised to hear some cicadas trying to sing on a rainy day one week ago. They didn't sound happy. Today, however, they are full of energy. It's going to be a noisy day.

weather forecaster　気象予報士　　cicada　セミ

 毎年セミの声が梅雨明けを告げます。僕の母国アメリカでは梅雨もないし，セミもあまり出ないので，この時期になると「日本だな！」と感じます。ごみごみした大都会でも自然界の力を感じます。

What Do You Call a Wine Specialist?

What do you call a wine specialist, a sommelier or a wine connoisseur? I said "sommelier" to an American, but he asked me what it meant. I told him that it is a person who knows wines and has a certificate to show that he or she is a wine specialist. A few days later, I said "sommelier" again. He had asked his family and some relatives, all of whom are American, if they knew the word. No one did. He thought that "sommelier" was probably a technical term in the world of wine. According to him, ordinary Americans call this person a "wine connoisseur" rather than a "sommelier."

(Written by a reader, Imai Takao)

specialist　専門家　　sommelier　ソムリエ　　connoisseur　専門家
certificate　認定証　　relative　親戚　　technical term　専門用語

Sommelier?   Wine connoisseur?

 「ソムリエ」はもともとフランス語からきています。アメリカでは，この職業自体が一般的ではないし，ソムリエは高級レストランでしか働きません。高級レストランに縁がない人は「ソムリエ」という言葉をあまり聞かないでしょうね。

Beating the Heat

The rainy season is officially over. Now it's time for the hot Japanese summer. I asked some adult students for ideas on how to beat the heat. Here are their suggestions: 1) use a parasol when you are outside, 2) wear light clothing, 3) use an electric fan or an air conditioner when you are inside, 4) drink lots of water and eat salt candy before exercising, 5) go swimming, 6) eat garlic after exercising to help your body recover from tiredness, 7) go and watch fireworks, and 8) eat shaved ice. Which do you do? Do you have any other suggestions?

officially　公式に　　suggestion　提案　　electric fan　扇風機
recover　回復する　　tiredness　疲労

 本当の暑さは梅雨明けからですね。水を飲んだり、塩あめをなめたりする対策のほかに、インドやタイのような暑い国での調理法も参考になるかもしれません。ニンニクやトウガラシで料理を辛くして食べると暑さに負けないようになるでしょう。

A Great Guinness Record

Ethiopia, a country in East Africa, has a problem. It is losing trees every year. The main reason is that there are more and more people living in the country. Ethiopia has the second largest population of any country in Africa. As the population grows, people cut down more trees for farming, and they use the wood for cooking and heating. This causes many environmental problems, so the government is trying to change things. On July 29, they closed public offices, and people all over Ethiopia planted more than 350 million saplings in one day. What a great Guinness record!

Ethiopia エチオピア   population 人口   public office 官公庁
sapling 苗木

エチオピア政府によると，7月29日に国民が全土で3億5千万本以上の木を植えました。干ばつや洪水に悩まされているエチオピアを植樹によって，土地の劣化や浸食から守る狙いがあります。この植樹プロジェクトが認定されれば，新記録としてギネスブックに載ります。

A New Star

Last night I kept checking online about the Women's British Open. I wanted to see how Shibuno Hinako was doing in her first golf tournament outside Japan. Shibuno is known as the "Smiling Cinderella" in Japan, but she was unknown to the outside world. What a surprise! She was playing with the world's best golfers, and she was in the lead at the end of three days. I sat at my computer and was reading the live updates. She went down to second place. Then she was tied for first. Finally, she won the tournament by one stroke! She is a new star in the golf world.

in the lead　首位に立って　　live update　生中継の最新情報
one stroke　1打

「スマイルシンデレラ」と呼ばれる渋野日向子選手が
AIG全英女子オープンで優勝しました。海外の大
会に初出場した彼女は無名選手でしたが，最終日の
トップ争いでも「スマイル」を見せ続け，地元のイギ
リス人にも応援されるようになりました。

Having a Good Time

Last week we were very busy at Fujimae Tidal Flat in Nagoya. Why? Because of the new moon. When there is a new moon or a full moon, the tidal flat appears for a few hours each day. We plan special trips out onto the tidal flat on the weekend, and on weekdays schools and other groups come to Fujimae. The temperature was over 35 degrees centigrade every day, but we didn't feel so hot walking around on the flat. We made holes in the mud and found a lot of small fish, crabs, and clams. Everyone had a good time, especially the children.

tidal flat　干潟　　appear　現れる　　mud　泥　　clam　二枚貝

 潮干狩りを経験した人は分かると思いますが，干潟が広く露出するのは満月や新月の大潮の時だけです。真夏の暑い日でも干潟の上にいれば猛暑を忘れられます。子どもは生きもの探しに夢中になり，新しい発見がたくさんあります。

"The Bluest Eye"

I remember reading a book called "The Bluest Eye" years ago. It made a strong impression on me. The story is about a black girl. People around her say that she is ugly, but she wants to be beautiful. She has a doll with blue eyes and dreams of having the same beautiful blue eyes as the doll. This novel was the first book written by Toni Morrison, a famous American writer. Morrison went on to write more than 10 novels and win the Nobel Prize in Literature in 1993. She passed away on Monday at the age of 88.

impression　印象　　ugly　醜い
the Nobel Prize in Literature　ノーベル文学賞

アメリカの黒人女性は 1960 年代まで「美しい」とされていませんでした。当時「美」は白人のものと考えられていました。この小説の主人公は黒人の少女で青い目にあこがれていました。差別や偏見が彼女の強いあこがれを生んだのです。

I Can't Help Eating Eel

I eat *una-ju* to keep up my strength in summer. My family buys it at Lawson every year because my sister works there part-time. She brings home an advertisement, we see it, and then we feel like eating eel. These days, food waste is becoming a problem. Actually, my sister sometimes talks about it at home. I'm surprised to hear that they have to throw food away even a couple of days before the expiration date. I usually order the biggest *una-ju* called *tokujo*. Thinking about food waste, I promise to finish eating all of it!

(Written by a reader, Kawasaki Naomi)

---

eel　うなぎ　　advertisement　広告
food waste　食品廃棄物，食品の無駄　　expiration date　賞味期限

コンビニでうなぎを売っているということには驚きます。うなぎは安ければ完売するでしょう。弁当やおでんのような食べ物は時間が経つと食品廃棄物になります。便利さを保ちながら，食品の無駄をどう減らすかがコンビニの課題ですね。

Taking Care of a Pet

My daughter and her family are in Hokkaido now, so I am taking care of their pet. It's a small bird called a parakeet. I don't have to do much. I just change the water every day. The bird's name is Sky, so I think you can guess what color he is. That's right! He's light blue. Male birds often repeat what their owners say, but I haven't heard Sky talk yet. He does make a chirping noise. I'm trying to teach him "Sky is cute" in English, but he still only speaks bird language. He is friendly and likes to sit on my head or shoulder. He enjoys pulling my hair with his beak.

parakeet　セキセイインコ（イギリス英語では budgerigar）
male　オスの　　chirping noise　鳥がさえずる音
beak　くちばし

今まで犬や猫は飼ったことがありますが，鳥を飼ったことはありませんでした。「スカイ」を一時的に預かったときは新鮮な気持ちでした。愛想のいい子ですが，一回大変な目に遭いました。納戸にぶら下がっている服の中に入って，しばらく出てきませんでした。

Yukatas

We can see many people wearing yukatas at summer festivals, mainly when they go to see the fireworks. In the old days, people wore their yukatas every day in summer. People wore them until the yukatas wore out. Then, people made dusters and diapers out of them. When I was young, my mother made several yukatas for me. But by that time, people didn't wear them so often. My yukatas were sleeping in my chest of drawers for a long time, so this summer I decided to make summer blouses out of them. I made two blouses. These blouses are more comfortable and cooler than regular clothes.

(Written by a reader, Ito Hiromi)

wore　wear の過去形　　wear out　すり切れる
duster　ふきん，ぞうきん　　diaper　おむつ
chest of drawers　たんす

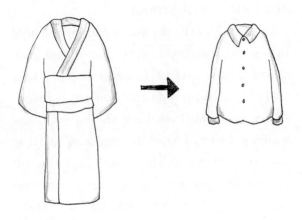

日本の「もったいない」文化は，物が豊富でなかった
時代に生まれたのでしょう。服をそのまま捨てない
で，再利用する人は多いと思います。僕の妻も着古
した綿のＴシャツを切って，ぞうきんに再利用し
ています。

The First Day of School

My sister works at an elementary school in her neighborhood. The new school year starts at the end of summer in the U.S., and this Monday was the first day. I went to see the school with my sister. As I was walking home, I saw the children arriving with their parents. The school yard was full of excited children and adults. Everyone was saying hello and talking to friends. Some of the children came on foot, but many rode bicycles or scooters. There were no long speeches. The teachers got the children into groups and took them inside to their new classrooms. They had a full day of classes.

neighborhood　近所　　school yard　校庭，グラウンド
adult　大人

アメリカの学校では始業式はありません。校長先生がスピーチをすることがなく，初日も朝から授業があります。アメリカ人の僕が日本の学校で不思議に思うことは，初日は式があるだけで授業がないことです。授業がないならば，なぜ学校へ行かなければならないのか分かりません。

3+8 = CHEAP!

I happened to eat miso ramen at the Ramen Sanpachi restaurant in Atsubetsu, Sapporo, on August 3. March 8 is called "Sanpachi Day," and you can eat six kinds of ramen cheaper than usual on that day. That is because 3 (the third month) is "*san*" and 8 is "*hachi*" in Japanese. When "*san*" and "*hachi*" are put together, they are pronounced "*sanpachi*." March 8 is the ordinary Sanpachi Day, but August 3 is called "Ura Sanpachi Day," or "Reverse Sanpachi Day." When I went on August 3, I only paid 410 yen for miso ramen. I even got a free ice candy bar when I left the restaurant.

(Written by a reader, Shinya Norimasa)

happen to ～　たまたま～する　　ordinary　普通の

 ラーメンさんぱちの店名の由来は，創業時の社長の年齢のようです。38歳で1号店を作って，北海道ではすごい勢いで店舗を増やしました。天候を考えると3月より8月に北海道へ食べに行きたいと思いますが，ちょっと遠すぎますね。

Labor Day Is BBQ Day in the U.S.

Today is a public holiday called Labor Day in the U.S. "Labor" means "work," so this is a day to celebrate workers. Most workers don't get together for labor events like they do on May 1, 2019 in Japan. People just think of Labor Day as the end of the summer vacation and enjoy their last chance to relax. The holiday always falls on a Monday, so they have a 3-day weekend. According to one website, 41% of Americans have barbecues at this time. That sounds about right. Both of my sister's children had barbecues over the weekend.

Labor Day　レイバー・デー(労働者の日)
BBQ = barbecue　　fall on ～　(曜日)にあたる

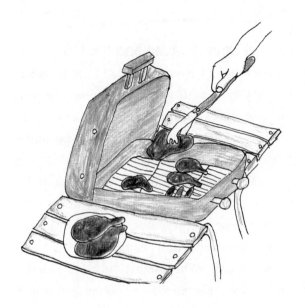

僕が通っていた学校では，レイバー・デーが終わってから授業が始まりましたが，州によってはレイバー・デーより前に授業が始まるところもあります。でも連休は連休なので，バーベキューは定番ですね。日本では学校が始まる直前は，宿題に追われているので，家族と出かけることは考えられないでしょう。

Special Days in Japan and the U.S.

November 11 is written 11/11. It is called Pocky Day because the date looks like thin Pocky sticks. The number 29 can be read as "*niku*," so the 29th of each month becomes "Meat Day." My nephew told me that the same thing happens in the U.S. March 14 is 3/14. It is called Pi Day because 3.14 is very close to the value of Pi (π) in math. Can you guess what people do on Pi Day? They eat pie! What about July 11? That's right. It's 7-Eleven Day. You can get a free frozen drink from that convenience store in the U.S.

nephew おい   be close to the value 値に近い

π

英語で語呂合わせを作るのは日本語ほど簡単ではありませんが，英語でも語呂合わせに似たものがあります。アメリカのセブン - イレブンでは7月11日にSlurpee（スラーピー）というシャーベット状の炭酸飲料を安くしたり，無料で配ったりするキャンペーンがあります。

A New Way to Get around Cities

Most cities have buses and taxis, and some have subways. In the last 10 or 15 years, some cities have started renting bicycles. Now there is a new way to get around: electric scooters. A lot of people are using them in and around Washington, D.C. First, you have to go online and rent them. Then you use your cell phone Wi-Fi to find the scooters. People ride them on sidewalks and in the street. They can travel up to 16 kilometers per hour. When riders are finished, they just leave the scooters on the sidewalk. They look like fun to ride, but I wonder if they are safe.

electric scooter　電動キックボード　　sidewalk　歩道

2019年の夏にニューヨークへ行った時，電動キックボードはまったく見かけませんでしたが，その直後に行ったワシントン D.C. ではどこにでもありました。時速 16 キロで走る電動キックボードなのに，誰もヘルメットをかぶっていなかったのは気になりました。

American Japanese Reminds Me of Japanese English

My daughter in Virginia moved into a new apartment at the end of July. She only had stuffed chairs, but she wanted a sofa that could be used as a bed. I decided to buy one for her birthday. She found one that she really liked. It is called a "futon" in the U.S. It has a Japanese name, but it is very different from a Japanese *futon*. It has a metal frame, and you can put the back up and sit on it like a sofa. If you let the back down, you can make a flat bed. Why do Americans use a Japanese word for this kind of sofa? I don't know, but American Japanese reminds me of Japanese English.

remind A of ～　A に～を思い出させる
metal frame　金属製の骨組み

外来語は必ずしも元の言葉の意味のまま使い続けるとは限りません。futon という言葉は日本語から来ていますが、「布団」とは違います。寝床として使えるので布団の役割は持っていますが、futon は布団ではありません。

"It Came Too Soon!"

I saw Ohno Yudai of the Chunichi Dragons jumping up and down at the end of the game with the Hanshin Tigers last Saturday. He pitched a no-hitter. He is only the 81st pitcher in the history of Japanese baseball to do it. He was so happy that he couldn't control his joy. He thanked his teammates saying that a no-hitter is not possible without them. A lot of fans sent him e-mails, but one e-mail came from another pitcher, Softbank's Senga Kodai. His message said, "It came too soon!" Senga had done it just eight days before.

no-hitter　ノーヒットノーラン（無安打無得点試合）
control one's joy　喜びを抑える

僕は中日ファンなので，大野投手のノーヒットノーランは知っていましたが，ソフトバンクの千賀投手が最近ノーヒットノーランを達成したばかりだとは知りませんでした。千賀投手から大野投手に「達成するの早すぎです」というメールが届いたようです。冗談半分にしても，主役を奪われた本音がうかがえますね。

Cycling to the World Cup

The Rugby World Cup will start in Tokyo this Friday. Two men are coming from Britain, but they aren't traveling by airplane. They are coming on their bicycles. That is a 20,000-kilometer trip! Ron Rutland and James Owens left London in February, and they have been cycling towards Japan ever since. Why are they doing this? They want to make money for a charity, and they want to teach people across Asia about rugby. They have cycled through Europe, Iran and India. Now they are in Japan after taking a ferry from Shanghai to Osaka.

charity 慈善事業, チャリティー

 世界にラグビーのことをもっと知ってもらうために，2人の男性が自転車でヨーロッパとアジアを横断してラグビーワールドカップの開催国である日本へやってきました。実はこの2人がワールドカップの開幕戦である日本対ロシア戦で使う笛を運んできたのです。間に合ってよかったです！

Like an Amusement Park

People are always surprised when I say I like going to the dentist. I explain it like this: "The dental clinic is like an amusement park. There is a very comfortable reclining chair. Sitting in it and listening to the sound of the dentist's drill can be a thrilling moment. No one is trying to kill you. If you like a roller coaster, you should like the dentist, too." This spring I had to go to the dentist for a cavity. That was a happy time for me. Now I am looking forward to getting a notice of the next check-up.

(Written by a reader, Satsuta Manami)

dentist　歯医者　　thrilling　わくわくさせる　　cavity　虫歯
get a notice　通知を受け取る

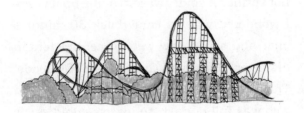

正直にいうと，僕には歯科医院を遊園地に例える読者の気持ちは分かりかねます。ジェットコースターは好きですが，歯の治療を受けるために椅子に座ると，わくわくするのではなく，体が震えてしまいます。いつ痛みがくるかと考えながら，心を落ち着かせようとします。

A Spider at a Hot Spring

I saw something wonderful in an open-air hot spring. A spider was breaking up its web. I wondered why. I came back 30 minutes later and saw a new web 40 centimeters in diameter. I counted the number of threads. The web had 45 threads! I thought the old web was full of dust, so insects could easily find it. The spider knew that and made a new web again. How clever it is! I was so excited that I watched from the bath for a long time and my body became red like a boiled octopus.

(Written by a reader, Kitahara Nobuaki)

open-air hot spring　露天の温泉　　web　クモの巣
diameter　直径　　thread　糸

この読者は露天風呂に入っているときに，クモが古い巣を壊しているのを見つけました。クモの巣の糸を数えるとは観察力がたくましいですね。彼は我を忘れて，観察を続けていたため，長風呂で体が真っ赤になってしまいました。

Dog Food and People Food

At 12:01 a.m. today the consumption tax went up in Japan. I went to a convenience store after midnight to check the new prices. A clerk was talking to a customer and said, "When I came into work, I remembered that the tax was going up tonight. It's such a pain!" I think he had to change all the prices in the store. Luckily for him, the tax was still 8% on food, candy and non-alcoholic drinks. One kind of food was more expensive. The tax on dog food is 10%. One of my wife's friends has a dog. He said that his dog is getting too expensive to keep, so he is going to send it out to work.

consumption tax　消費税　　pain　わずらわしいこと
non-alcoholic　ノンアルコールの
send 〜 out to work　〜を働きに行かせる

 消費税は複雑になりましたね。人間の食べ物は8％のままですが，ペットフードは10％に上がります。もちろん妻の友達が飼い犬を働かせるわけはありませんが，えさ代は高くなるでしょう。買い物客よりも惑わされるのは店員でしょう。

It Made Me Smile

I was looking at an online weather report last night. I wanted to know if I could travel by bicycle or if I would have to take the subway. I scrolled down the page. The forecast said that there was only a 10% chance of rain after 6 a.m. That made me happy. Below that was a list of things connected to the weather. It said that there was a 50% chance of drying clothes outside, but they told us to bring umbrellas. We had to be careful of heat stroke, but they said it could be too cool to wear a polo shirt. The last thing made me smile. There was a 50% chance that we would want to drink beer!

weather report　天気予報　　scroll down　下へスクロールする
(be) connected to ～　～と関係のある　　heat stroke　熱中症

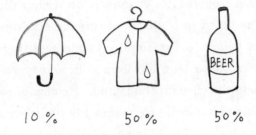

10%   50%   50%

 天気予報のサイトは情報が豊かですね。暑い時に
ビールを飲みたくなる確率を載せるのは賛成です！
ビールが嫌いな僕の妻はきっとそう思わないでしょ
う。逆に，春になると花粉症に悩まされる妻は，花
粉飛散情報を注意深く見ますが，僕には関係ありま
せん。

A Great 300-Year-Old Adventure Novel

Do you know "Robinson Crusoe"? It is a novel from 1719. A man is on a ship that goes down in a storm. Everyone else dies, but he gets to an island. No one lives there. He makes a tent and lives in it, and he eats goats that live on the island. He also grows some of his food. He makes his own clothes with leather from the goats. He lives on the island for 28 years until he is rescued. This is fiction, but at that time there were real people who survived alone on islands far from Britain. This book was very popular when it came out, and it is still one of the most famous books in English.

Robinson Crusoe　ロビンソン・クルーソ　　rescue　救助する
survive　生き残る

この小説がベストセラーになったのは，現実味が
あったからでしょう。300年前，イギリスの船は全
世界を航海していて，遠く離れた太平洋に行った船
の中には遭難して帰ってこないものもありました。
実際に無人島で数年間生き残って助けられた人もい
ました。

Lithium Leads to the Nobel Prize

Yoshino Akira has won the Nobel Prize in Chemistry together with John B. Goodenough and M. Stanley Whittingham. The three scientists were given the prize for their research on the lithium battery. This battery has changed the world. Older batteries were weaker, and they were much bigger. Lithium batteries are strong and much smaller, and they can be recharged many times. They power many things such as mobile phones, laptops, and electric cars. Thanks to discoveries by Whittingham and Goodenough, Yoshino was able to create the first workable lithium battery.

lithium battery　リチウム電池　　recharge　（再）充電する
power　電力を供給する　　laptop　ノートパソコン
workable　（実際に）使える

2019年のノーベル化学賞は，私たちの生活に欠かせないリチウムイオン電池の開発に重要な役割を果たした3人に贈られました。科学者の発見を共有することによって，知識が蓄積し，進歩につながります。目標をもって研究しても，計画通りに進む学者ばかりではありません。研究課題は好奇心に任せることも大事です。

Chris the Sheep

Chris, a Merino sheep who is in the Guinness World Records, has died. He was 10 years old. He was a famous sheep, but how did he become famous? Merino sheep are raised for wool. Their wool needs to be sheared every year, but no one ever cut off Chris's wool. When he was found in the wild in 2015, he looked like a big, dirty cloud on legs. They cut off Chris's wool and weighed it. A normal sheep's fleece weighs about 5 kilograms, but Chris's fleece weighed more than 40 kilograms. It was almost half his weight! No wonder he got into the Guinness Book!

raise　飼育する　　shear　刈る　　fleece　（1匹分の）羊毛

オーストラリアの羊の多くはメリノ種です。毎年必ず1回毛を刈る必要がある種ですが，迷子になったクリスは5年以上刈ってもらえなくて，身動きが取れなくなるほど毛が重くなってしまいました。首都キャンベラ市にあるオーストラリア国立博物館へ行けば，刈られた羊毛が見られます。

A Pot of Salmon Roe

My son went to the local fish processing factory for his junior high school work experience program. He wanted to work as a shop assistant, and he chose the place because the name was Nishiya Shoten. "*Shoten*" is a retail store in Japanese. He thought he would sell something at the store, but it turned out to be a fish factory. He had to process salmon and take out the roe (fish eggs). He worked so hard that he was given a large amount of salmon roe when he left the factory. It filled a medium-sized cooking pot. It was a tough day for him, but we were very lucky to eat lots of salmon and roe.

(Written by a reader, Shinya Norimasa)

fish processing factory　水産加工工場
work experience program　職業体験　　retail store　小売店
turn out to be ～　　～であることがわかる

この中学生は職業体験の日に出勤して驚いたに違い
ありません。名前だけで判断するのではなく，ちゃ
んと下調べすべきだとこれで覚えたでしょう。今回
得たものはそれだけではなく，おいしいものがもら
えて，家族を喜ばせることができたのが何より良
かったですね。

Uluru Is Closed to Climbers

Uluru (also known as Ayers Rock) is a mountain-like rock in the middle of Australia. The Anangu are the people who have lived around the rock for over 10,000 years. Uluru has a very special place in Anangu culture, and the Anangu believe that no one should climb it. For many years, however, tourists did not listen to them and kept climbing Uluru. Finally, two days ago, Uluru was closed to climbers. You can no longer hike to the top, but don't worry. You can still get a beautiful view of Uluru from the bottom and take a helicopter ride to get a wider view of the area.

view 景色

ウルルはシドニーから飛行機で3時間半，車で30時間もかかりますが，人気の観光地です。赤い一枚岩が，平らな砂漠の大地から800メートル以上の高さでそびえ立っています。朝日がこの巨大な岩に当たる様子を写真に収めるのはお勧めです。

Goodbye to a Great Woman

Ogata Sadako has passed away. She did many things in her life, but I remember her when she was working for the United Nations. She was in charge of helping refugees from 1991 to 2000. There were many refugees all over the world when she started her work. Because of wars in many parts of the world, people were leaving their countries to look for safety. Some people stayed in their countries but had to move away from their homes. She worked very hard to make sure that all these people were safe.

pass away　亡くなる　　the United Nations　国際連合, 国連
refugee　難民

 流暢な英語で演説をする緒方貞子さんは，本当に国際的な視点から物事を考える人でした。大学の教授，学部長の職を経て，国連で難民問題に取り組みました。多くの人の命を救った緒方さんは次のように述べていました。「難民を受け入れることは，日本を含めた世界全体の人材育成に繋がることを忘れてはならないと思います。」

A Halloween Quiz

It's Halloween today. I have a quiz for you.

(1) In which country did the holiday originate?

(2) What was the original name of Halloween? (3 words)

(3) What vegetable was first used to make a jack o'lantern?

(4) What do children wear at Halloween?

(5) What do people give children at Halloween?

(6) What is the name of the movie about a creature from outer space with a Halloween scene in it?

originate　始まる　　creature　生きもの　　outer space　宇宙

このクイズに対して解答を寄せた7人中4人が満点でした。最近日本人の子どもがハロウィンをするようになりました。そのせいか，日本人もハロウィンについてずいぶん詳しくなっています。

答え (1) Ireland. (2) All Hallow's Eve. (3) The turnip. (4) Costumes. (5) Candies and other sweets. (6) "E.T."

You're in Paradise

My wife was driving from Washington, D.C. to Pennsylvania to meet a friend. She got lost and decided to ask for directions. She stopped at a furniture store. When she asked the owner where she was, he said, "Paradise." "Paradise" has the same meaning as "heaven." My wife thought he was kidding and said, "Don't I wish!" but the man looked at her seriously. "You are in Paradise. This is Paradise Furniture Store." She looked out and checked the sign. He was right. She was in a city called "Paradise." Actually, Pennsylvania has some of the most unusual city names of any state in the U.S.

---

paradise　天国　　furniture store　家具店　　kid　冗談を言う
Don't I wish! = I wish (I were in Paradise).　（自分が）天国にいたらいいのに。

ペンシルベニア州には面白い地名がいっぱいあります。例えば, Bird-in-Hand（手中の鳥）, Gravity（重力）, King of Prussia（プロイセンの王）, Moon（月）, Panic（パニック）, Two Lick Valley（2度舐めの渓谷）などです。

Are All Japanese Ghosts Female?

When I think of Japanese ghosts, I only think of women and girls. For example, there is a ghost called Kuchisake-onna. She wears a mask to hide her terrible face, but if you say that she isn't beautiful, she will kill you. There is a ghost of a girl in the school restroom. Her name is Hanako-san, and children believe that she pulls them into the toilet. Then there is Okiku, a beautiful servant. Her master killed her, so her ghost came back to haunt him. Sadako is a ghost in the book and movie, "Ring." I can think of many female ghosts but no male ghosts. Are all Japanese ghosts female?

ghost 幽霊, おばけ　　female 女性の　　servant 召使い
haunt つきまとう, とりつく

白い着物を着ている女性の顔に長い髪がかかり，足がない姿。これが僕の日本のおばけのイメージです。「うらめしや」と言いながら，生きている人の前に現れます。「リング」に出てくる貞子は世界的に有名になりました。

There Are Male Ghosts, Too!

There are also male ghosts in Japan, but we don't know many because they only appear in a few pictures. One of the most famous male ghosts is Sugawara Michizane. He is a well-known person in Japanese history. He was sent away from Kyoto, the capital of Japan, even though he did nothing wrong. He was sent to Dazaifu in Kyushu and died there. He became a ghost after his death because of the bad feelings he had towards his enemies in Kyoto. He is said to have cursed and killed those who made him go to Dazaifu. I think that this story is more realistic than the stories of female ghosts.

(Written by a reader, Kawase Noh)

male　男性の　　capital　首都　　curse　のろいをかける

 数年前に僕は家族と一緒に京都へ行き，北野天満宮を訪れました。その時に初めて菅原道真が学問の神様だと知りましたが，こんな悲劇的な人生を送った人だとは思いもしませんでした。

Not a Cat Café

   You have probably heard of cat cafés. They seem to be very popular, especially among young women. Now there are places where you can touch and hold other kinds of animals. I was walking around the downtown area of Nagoya the other day, and I saw a young woman standing on the corner with a large owl on her arm. It had big orange eyes. I asked her what she was doing. She told me that she was handing out advertisements for an animal café. She said that I could hold the owl if I went there. According to her, they also had hawks, snakes, meerkats and hedgehogs! I think I'll check it out.

owl　フクロウ　　advertisement　広告　　hawk　タカ
meerkat　ミーアキャット　　hedgehog　ハリネズミ

猫や犬はペットとして飼いならされているから扱いやすいと思いますが，野生動物は扱いにくいと思います。狩りの習性を持つフクロウやタカ類は，人馴れしていても，鋭い爪で攻撃されないように注意が必要です。

A Fat Cat in the News

A fat cat named Viktor is in the news now. He belongs to a Russian man named Mikhail Galin. Galin wanted to take Viktor on a plane with him, but the cat was too heavy. Cats cannot be more than 8 kilograms, but Viktor weighed 10 kilograms. Galin borrowed a lighter cat and told the airline that it was Viktor. They let him take it on the plane. Before he got on the plane, however, Galin changed the cats and put Viktor in the carrier. Everything was okay until he posted the story and a photo on Facebook and Instagram. Aeroflot found out, and they canceled Galin's mileage points.

carrier　キャリーバッグ　　Aeroflot　アエロフロート・ロシア航空

猫の替え玉事件ですね！　大切なペットと離れたくない飼い主の気持ちは分かりますが，航空会社のルールを破ったのを得意気にSNSに投稿することは理解できません。ガリンさんのマイレージポイントを取り消した航空会社の対応は当然です。

Ville, Burgh and Town

Many cities in English-speaking countries end with "ville" and "burgh." Do you know why? "Ville" means "town" or "city" in French. My daughter once lived in a city called Charlottesville. It was named after the wife of King George III of Britain. "Burg" or "burgh" means "fort" or "castle," and cities in Europe were named after their castles, like Edinburgh, Scotland, and Salzburg, Austria. There are cities which are named after forts in the U.S. such as Pittsburgh, Pennsylvania. There are also places that end in "town" such as Jamestown, the first English village in North America.

King George III　ジョージ 3 世　　castle　城

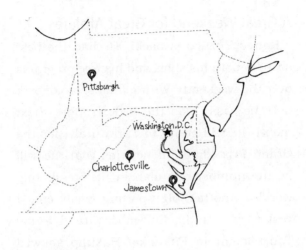

アメリカの植民地時代には，東海岸の入植地にイギリス本国の王室にちなんだ地名が付けられました。アメリカがイギリスから独立したら，王室は関係なくなり，自由な発想で地名を付けるようになりました。(Nov. 12 の "You're in Paradise" を参照)

A Great Weekend for Great Athletes

Hanyu Yuzuru is back! He had the best score in both his short and his free programs over the weekend. With a final score of over 300, he easily won the NHK Trophy. Next month he will go on to Turin, Italy, for the Grand Prix Final. If he wins that, he will be the number one man in the ice-skating world. Another big sporting event ended yesterday. At the November Grand Sumo Tournament in Fukuoka, Hakuho showed that he is still a champion. He finished the tournament with a record of 14-1, three wins ahead of any other wrestler. What a career! This is his 43rd tournament win.

　2人の選手は数年前のように無敵ではないけれど、今でも素晴らしい成績を残しています。他の選手を見ている時のような不安を感じさせないし、完璧に近い技術を見せてくれます。何度も優勝しており、この2人には引退の気配はありません。

Thanksgiving in the U.S.

Today is Thanksgiving in the U.S. On this day, families get together and have a big meal together. They celebrate this day to remember the first people who came from England to live in northeastern America. Those people had a very difficult first winter, but in the spring, they planted corn and other crops with the help of the native Americans (Indians). In the fall, they had a good harvest, and they held a three-day feast to thank God. They invited the native Americans to share their food. Wild deer and turkey were served at the feast, and that is why we eat turkey on Thanksgiving even today.

plant　植える　　crop　農作物　　harvest　収穫
feast　ごちそう

"Thanksgiving"という言葉は"give thanks"から来ています。約400年前にアメリカにたどり着いたイギリス人は，アメリカ先住民の協力により，厳しい冬を乗り越え，収穫の時に感謝の気持ちを込めて豊作を祝いました。今では，家族中心で祝うようになっています。

Buzzwords for 2019, but Don't Shout!

The buzzwords for this year have been announced. The first prize went to ONE TEAM. It was the slogan for the Brave Blossoms, Japan's rugby team. Their success came from working hard together. I think it is a great choice, but as an English teacher, I wish that they would write it as "One Team." When you write something all in capital letters, it doesn't look right. In fact, when you write in capital letters in SNS messages, it is called "shouting." It bothers me, and I think it bothers many native English users. Unfortunately, I see a lot of shouting when my students write.

buzzword　流行語　　shout　叫ぶ　　capital letter　大文字
bother　〜を嫌な思いにさせる

ONE TEAM

↓

One Team

 大文字ばかりの英単語は原則的に省略語ですね。SNS は Social Networking Service の省略ですし，US は United States の省略です。Who are you? は「だれですか？」とたずねる普通の言い方ですが，大文字ばかりの WHO ARE YOU? は「お前は一体何者だ？」という風に受け取れます。

Greta, a Girl with a Message

Greta Thunberg is a high school student from Sweden. She went to a meeting in New York to talk about climate change in September. On December 3, she arrived back in Europe for another meeting in Madrid, Spain. She crossed the Atlantic Ocean in a yacht, and it took more than 2 weeks each way. Why didn't she fly? Because flying is bad for the environment. Airplanes use a lot of fuel and produce a lot of CO2. She sailed on a yacht which uses wind and solar power. She believes that people need to change their lifestyles to stop climate change.

climate change　気候変動　　the Atlantic Ocean　大西洋
environment　環境　　lifestyle　生活様式

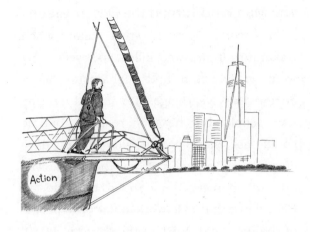

グレタ・トゥーンベリさんの話を聞いて，感動し，共感する人が多くいます。このスウェーデンの高校生が絶えず環境保護をアピールすることによって，世界中の人々の環境に対する考え方を変えたことは，グレタ効果と呼ばれています。

The Man Who Turned the Desert Green

The world lost a great man when Nakamura Tetsu was killed last week. He went to Pakistan and Afghanistan as a doctor many years ago. He started treating sick people, but he soon realized that he could not save people who didn't have enough food or water. Even though he was not an engineer, he decided to build an irrigation canal. He worked with the people of the area and finished the canal in 2010. Water came to a desert where people used to live. People returned to their villages, and when they started farming, the desert became green again.

desert 砂漠　　treat 治療する　　irrigation canal 灌漑用水路

 中村氏はもともと医師としてパキスタンへ派遣されましたが，アフガニスタンまで活動を広げました。現地では水不足による栄養不良が深刻なため，医療の前に水が必要だと考えて，灌漑用水路を作ったおかげで，乾いた土地が緑の畑になりました。

Living without a Cell Phone

How long can you live without a cell phone? I met a girl on Sunday who had to go without a phone for one year. She went to Australia in March at the end of her second year of junior high school. On her way back, she left her cell phone somewhere inside Changi Airport in Singapore. She didn't notice that it was missing until she got back to Japan. When she told her parents, they said that they wouldn't buy her another phone. She had to live without a phone for one year, but she said that it was a good experience because it helped her to concentrate on studying for her high school entrance exams.

go without 〜　〜なしでやっていく　　notice　気づく
missing　紛失した　　concentrate on 〜　〜に集中する

 携帯電話なしで1年も生活できる日本の中学生はほとんどいないと思います。この中学生にとってはきっとつらくて、一生忘れられない出来事だったでしょう。でも、僕が驚いたのは、本人が携帯がなくて良かった点を強調したことです。携帯がないおかげで勉強に集中できて良かったですね。

What I Miss about Christmas

I really miss singing Christmas carols. I grew up singing them, and when I am in the U.S., I can sing along with other people. In Japan, I have to sing by myself because hardly anyone knows the songs. Even if they know the melody, they don't know the English words. One of my favorite songs is called "O Holy Night." It is a very dramatic song about the night that Jesus Christ was born. Another song I like is very long. It's called "The Twelve Days of Christmas." On each day, someone gives their loved one another present. The presents get grander, and the song gets faster.

miss 　〜がないのをさみしく思う
carol 　（クリスマスの）聖歌，讃美歌
hardly anyone 〜　〜する人はほとんどいない
grander 　grand（豪華な）の比較級

日本ではクリスマスの歌を歌う機会はほとんどありませんが，欧米のクリスマスは歌と深い関係があります。そもそも教会では毎週日曜日に讃美歌や聖歌を歌います。キリストが生まれたことも歌で祝います。小さい時から歌い続けた僕は，歌詞を見ずに10曲以上歌えます。

The Songs That They Already Know

Yesterday was a special day for me. The university tap dance club that I coach had its Christmas performance. Many of the people who came to see us were former members of the club (OG). One came all the way from Hiroshima, and another came from Tokyo just to see our performance. At the end, we gave everyone questionnaires. One person talked about how good she felt when she heard a song that she had danced to many years before. I was happy that different people liked different dances. Of course, the dancing is important, but people usually prefer the songs that they already know.

former member　元メンバー　　questionnaire　アンケート

 大学のタップダンスクラブの年間最大のイベント
は，クリスマス発表会です。10月からの2か月間
に10曲ぐらい仕上げないといけません。もちろん
既に踊ったことのある曲もありますが，授業や実習
もやりながらよく頑張っていると思います。今回の
発表会にはたくさんのOGが来てくれて，励みにな
りました。

When the Moon Covers the Sun

Today is a special day around the world because there will be an eclipse of the sun. In Nagoya and Tokyo, the moon will cover 1/4 of the sun at about 3:30 this afternoon. It will probably get a little darker than usual, but you might not even notice the eclipse. If you want to see the full eclipse, you will need to go to Singapore. The people there will be able to see a ring of fire at about 1:24 in the afternoon. That happens when the moon is right in front of the sun. Wherever you are, be careful not to look directly at the sun. You will need special glasses to watch the eclipse.

cover　覆う　　eclipse of the sun　日食
ring of fire　金環日食のリング　　directly　直接に

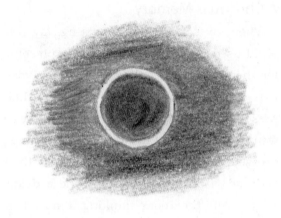

 この10年間に日本で見られる日食は6回ありました。そのうち，僕は2012年の金環日食に特に感動しました。近所の人と一緒に道に出て，特別なメガネを使って観察しました。皆既日食のように真っ暗にならなくて少しがっかりしましたが，月の周りから炎が見えた時には，その光景に満足しました。

A Christmas Memory

When my sons were very young, my wife and I used to talk about Christmas presents for them. We asked them about their wish lists for Santa Claus and prepared their presents secretly. One Christmas Eve, I went into their room with the presents, dressed as Santa Claus. It was after their bedtime. I put the presents at the bedside. Then I left the room thinking about their happy faces the next morning. But they only pretended to be asleep! They woke up immediately and were very happy. I asked them, "Did you see Santa Claus?" They said, "We saw him but couldn't see him clearly." I was lucky!

(Written by a reader, Ichikawa Nobuhiro)

wish list　欲しい物のリスト　　pretend to ～　～するふりをする
immediately　すぐに

この父親は本当に運が良かったです。サンタ姿で暗い寝室に忍び込んで，寝たふりをしている子どものベッドの横にプレゼントを置くことは，危険がいっぱいです。よくばれませんでした！

●著者略歴
Douglas S. Jarrell （ダグラス・ジャレル）
1953 年　アメリカ　ノースカロライナ州生まれ
大学の非常勤講師，藤前干潟の活動家

主な研究内容
• CALL（Computer-Assisted Language Learning,
　　コンピュータを利用した言語学習）
• 異文化コミュニケーション
など

表紙イラスト：たしろさなえ
本文イラスト：尾﨑香菜子
　　　　　　　梅村宏美
　　　　　　　Naomi Jarrell

じゃれマガ – 100 Stories of 2019
2020 年 6 月 1 日　初版第 1 刷発行

著者　　　ダグラス・ジャレル
発行元　　株式会社浜島書店
　　　　　〒 466-8691　名古屋市昭和区阿由知通 2-1-1
　　　　　電話 052（733）8040（代）

ISBN 978-4-8343 5046-3 C0082 ¥455E